HOT under the COLLAR

HOT under the COLLAR

MURRAY WATTS

MONARCH
Crowborough

First published 1992
Reprinted 1995

British Library Cataloguing in Publication Data

A catalogue record for this book is
available from the British Library.

ISBN 1-85424-195-8

Produced and printed in Great Britain for
Monarch Publications
Broadway House, The Broadway,
Crowborough, East Sussex TN6 1HQ by
Nuprint Ltd, Station Rd, Harpenden, Herts. AL5 4SE.

Acknowledgements

I cannot acknowledge everyone I would like to by name—so a general thank you, first of all, to anyone has prompted, inspired and helped to create this volume. A particular thank you, however, must go to the magnificent John Dixon of the Major Chuckle column, who has sent me nearly twenty items for this book. (Where Major Chuckle has been indebted to other sources, I have mentioned these in whatever detail possible.) John Dixon's enthusiasm and encouragement had a lot to do with persuading me to issue a successor to *Rolling in the Aisles* and *Bats in the Belfry*. In the latter, I erroneously referred to John as the Reverend John Dixon—however, I do think John deserves a title and it should probably be 'His Chuckleness' or 'The Right Ridiculous John Dixon'. Thank you, John, as ever.

A special thank you, too, to a real Reverend, Peter Lawrence who has contributed some true life stories in his own inimitable words.

The main people responsible for the publication of a third book are, of course, Tony and Jane Collins of Monarch—and I could not wish for more loving and appreciative editorial support.

I would also like to thank my friend Norman Stone, film-maker and director of 1A productions, who makes a rare switch to his alter ego as a cartoonist for this series of books. Another memorable cover, Norman, greatly appreciated.

Thanks are also due to Roger Royle and *Woman's Realm* magazine for permission to include an extract from 'The Royle Mail' column, the *Daily Mail* for the final entry, the calligrapher Stanford Hayward at Sudeley Castle in Gloucestershire, who drew my attention to a number of items in 'Wisecracks' with the beautifully written quips in his craft shop window.

The Priceless Pearls section draws upon howlers over the best part of the century, ranging from recent contributions to me, to Cecil Hunt's collections in the Thirties and even earlier in the American series of 'Boners'.

Thank you to my old friend Peter Bolton for permission to include one of his letters to me.

I am grateful as always to fellow members of Riding Lights Theatre Company, Paul Burbridge and Nigel Forde, Stuart Harrison and Richard Mapletoft among others, who are a generous source of wit and anecdote, and also to playwright Richard Everett whose quirky sense of humour has been one of the saving graces in my life. Very fond memories of the late Canon David Watson have surfaced often in writing this, as readers will readily appreciate when they see his name recurring.

I must also thank the Rev. Graham Cray, as one of

many friends who have told some excellent stories from the pulpit in recent years.

Thank you to my brother-in-law Paul Higginson, as well, who has one of the funniest turns of phrase I know and has always been an inspiration to me.

Thank you also to my wife Julie, who knows how to make people laugh both on and off stage—a rare gift.

My apologies to anyone, anywhere, who has a claim to be credited and has been inadvertently overlooked. Some material is sent to me without a provenance attached, often third or fourth hand transmissions, and of course many stories and incidents simply 'go the rounds'—so thank you to that famous raconteur and wit, 'Anon'.

There is an emphasis on children's humour in this book and so I would like to thank my two sons, Fionn and Toby, who are the ultimate inspiration for comedy in my life.

Finally, this book is affectionately dedicated to my beautiful god-daughters, Rebecca Suter, Joanna Harris, Hannah Cleverly and Rebecca Everett-Briggs—my thanks to them for brightening my life whenever I am lucky enough to see them.

CONTENTS

Foreword
Life After Birth
Preachers on Parade
Handle With Prayer
Filthy Lucre
The Laughter Clinic
Wisecracks
Clerical Errors
Priceless Pearls
Original Sins
For Better or For Worse
The Funny Side of Faith
The Twinkling of an Eye

Dedication

For Rebecca Suter, Joanna Harris, Hannah Cleverly and Rebecca Everett-Briggs.

Foreword

A child was once asked what she wanted more than anything else in the whole world. She said: 'The future.'

I am delighted that this third volume of jokes and stories is associated with The Children's Society, which is passionately committed to the present and future of so many children. There are many threats to peace today—not only to 'world peace' but to the peace of our inner worlds. Children, whose worlds are still forming, are the most at risk. I admire the enterprising vicar, collecting for The Children's Society, who stood in the local marketplace with the placard: 'Wife and 5,000 children to support.' I hope that readers of *Hot Under The Collar* will think up other imaginative ways to support the Society and invest in the future of our children.

But it is not only children who are dependent upon *us* for help, but we who are desperately dependent upon them. They can teach us how to laugh and how to live. The book of Proverbs—in one happy translation—describes wisdom as 'ever at play in the world.' It is truly wise to have fun. Perhaps the gravest error 'adults' can make is to think that they have nothing to learn from children. To listen to some people, you would think that every joke needs a justification and a book like this needs a reasoned theological defence. This is like saying that breathing requires an explanation before we can do it.

No defence is needed for humour—but its power in our lives is illuminated by the words of another little child: 'Perhaps laughter is a kind of prayer too.'

Murray Watts
September 1992

Life
After Birth

I remember a master at school saying to me, 'Are you trying to be awkward, boy?' 'No, sir,' I said, with perfect innocence. 'Well, you're succeeding very well without trying.' 'Thank you, sir,' I said. That was when he went berserk, for some reason. But it's quite true—no self-respecting child tries to be awkward. It's simply a matter of fulfilling one's potential— effortlessly—like the children who asked these questions at Sunday school:

'Why did the angels walk up and down Jacob's ladder, when they had wings and could fly?'

'But, Miss, didn't God love Goliath?'

Such questions are enough to give any Sunday school teacher a nervous breakdown.

———

1 A child was in church for the first time. Seeing all the adults kneeling on the cushions, she whispered to her mother: 'What are we hiding from?'

2 Another mother decided to start going to St Matthew's Church. She took her four-year-old son with her. At first, the little boy was nervous of the church and especially of the vicar, who had long hair, a beard and a booming voice. But he was a very good speaker and always entertained the children. Soon the little boy was looking forward eagerly to the Sunday morning services.

One Sunday he was utterly bewildered to find that the vicar was away and instead there was a clean-shaven and rather dull guest speaker.

'Oh, Mummy,' he whispered, 'whatever's happened to St Matthew?'

3 A divinity teacher was explaining the Creation story to his class. One awkward little boy—always a thorn in his side—called out: 'Please sir, my father says we are descended from the apes.' But this time the teacher was ready for him.

'Carruthers,' he snapped, 'your family problems are no concern of ours.'

With children, there are problems right from the word 'go'. As the comedian said:

> *'I was born at home. It was when my mother saw me she was taken to hospital.'*

Or:

> *'When I was born, the midwife took one look at me and slapped my mother.'*

According to psychiatrists, the first six months of our lives determine many things—in which case, my sister has something to worry about. When she was only a few weeks old, my father tripped on the top stair and lobbed her all the way down. My uncle Hilbre, a GP, happened to be standing in the hall at the time. As my sister lay there, bawling her head off, he scarcely looked up. 'It's only when they don't cry you need to worry,' he said. (Uncle Hilbre was always calm in the face of a crisis. It was he who said, 'Watch this for precision driving' before wedging his car between two trams in the city centre of Liverpool).

I suppose my father could have given the ultimate response to my sister's tumble: 'Come quickly, dear, our little girl's just taken her first twenty-five steps!'

4 A young couple, who had many financial difficulties, found themselves facing another pregnancy. They already had three boys and so a fourth child was considered a disaster by the husband. However, his wife comforted him with the possibility of a little daughter—this pregnancy 'felt different'.

She decided to make the birth as special as possible and have the baby at home. Husband and midwife were in attendance and, sure enough, the pregnancy was different. Very different. She had twins. Needless to say, they were both boys.

A little while later, the midwife went downstairs and met three-year-old George, up till then 'the baby of the family'. She explained to him that he now had two new little brothers.

'Oh,' said George nonchalantly, 'I know all about them.' 'Really?' said the nurse. 'Yes, and I know their *names* too.' 'Oh now,' said the midwife, smiling, 'you can't possibly know their names yet.' 'Oh, I do,' said George. 'I heard Daddy coming down the stairs saying "Hell and Damnation!" '

5 A sweet little girl of three knocked her six-year-old brother out with a punch. Her mother gasped in horror. 'Katie! How *could* you do such a thing?'

'The Lord gave me strength,' replied Katie proudly.

6 Teacher: 'Now, Jenny, can you tell me the name of a well-known animal that supplies us with food and clothing?'

Jenny: 'Yes. Daddy.'

7 A clergyman was taking tea with the farmer's wife when her children rushed in with a cardboard box.

'Mum!' they shouted triumphantly. 'We've trapped the rat!'

'Is it dead?' she asked anxiously.

'Oh, it's dead all right,' said the youngest boy. 'We beat it and beat it and beat it until—' Suddenly he noticed the clergyman's disapproving gaze. 'Until—er—' his voice dropped to a whisper, 'until the Lord called it home.'

8 A father was taking his thirteen-year-old to task for smoking in the garden shed.

'And what about you,' he said, turning to his ten-year-old daughter. 'Have you been smoking too?'

'No, Daddy,' she said, with righteous indignation. 'I certainly have not. I have given it up.'

9 Visit your mother today. Maybe she hasn't had any problems lately. *(Graffiti)*

John Dixon, editor of the Major Chuckle column, has sent me the following four stories:

10 A young lad was becoming rather restless during a church service. His mother leaned down: 'Ssssh,' she said, 'this is God's House.'

'Well,' said the boy, 'if I were God, I'd move.'

(Major Chuckle, quoting John Drew, 'Look at Life' in The Methodist Recorder*)*

11 Looking for the word 'Hallelujah', a preacher asked, 'What word do church members shout with joy?'

'Bingo!' replied one youngster.

(Major Chuckle, quoting Phil Mason, Christian Crackers, *Vol II, Norheimsund Books and Cards)*

12 A bishop was coming to stay at a vicar's house for the night. The vicar had an eight-year-old son, who was very excited about the important guest and begged his father to allow him to take the bishop his tea in the morning.

Eventually the vicar agreed, but told his son that he

must knock on the door and say, 'It's the boy, my Lord. It's time to get up.'

On his way upstairs the nervous boy was clutching the cup and saucer and practising the words his father had given him.

He knocked on the door and the bishop asked, 'Who is it?'

The boy replied at the top of his voice, 'It's the Lord, my boy. Your time is up!'

13 A speaker at a Harvest Family Service asked the children to name some of the things they saw on display.

'Carrots,' said one. 'Potatoes,' said another. 'Peas,' said a third.

'Good,' said the speaker. 'Now can anyone give me a word that covers all these things?'

'Gravy!' was the prompt reply.

---

14 The rector of All Hallows had newly arrived in the parish. He watched enthusiastically as his youth group practised on the village green for the final of a cricket tournament, but he was horrified to see how ill-equipped they were—bats cracked and bandaged, stumps old and rotten, leather ball coming apart, pads dirty and torn. The boys were amazed when he gave them £100 of his own money towards new equipment.

A few weeks later, the rector arrived at the match with eager anticipation. The All Hallows Youth Club won and he cheered loudly, but he was perplexed to see them playing with the same old tattered stuff.

'What happened to the money I gave you?' he asked.

'Well, Reverend,' the young captain explained, 'you told us to spend the money on bats, balls, gloves, or anything that might help us win the game. So we gave the £100 to the umpire.'

15 I can't help admiring one little boy who summed up the problems of evil memorably. His pious grandmother caught him beating up his sister.

'Billy,' she said, leaning over him and shaking her finger, 'it was Satan who told you to scratch Catherine's face!'

'Perhaps it was,' said Billy, 'but it was *my* idea to kick her in the shins.'

16 Life was peaceful in the Morgan family until the invention of video games. All the neighbours' children now had Nintendo or Sega computers. The pressure on Richard and Michael Morgan, nine and seven years old, was overwhelming, but the parents stood firm. Children's TV and Thundercats they could just about stand; Star Wars videos were allowed to shatter the calm on occasion; but the jingles and maddening little bleeps of Sonic the Hedgehog: No, no. And no again.

Richard Morgan accepted the inevitable, but Michael was persistent. At bedtime his prayers changed from 'God bless Mummy and Daddy and help all the poor people in the world' to anguished pleadings for a Sega Megadrive.

'O dear Lord, please, please, send me one. I promise I'll be good for ever.'

This went on for some weeks until his mother gently took the situation in hand.

'Michael,' she said, 'you shouldn't just pray for things you covet. There's more to prayer than wanting expensive new toys—the Lord wants to hear about other things too.'

For a while, Michael took the advice to heart. He prayed quite meekly and kindly for others, sick relatives, the poor and needy. But one night, the children were praying alone and Richard suddenly rushed down stairs. 'Mum! Mum! Come quickly!'

'What is it?' asked his mother.

'It's serious,' said Richard. 'Michael's worrying the Lord about that Sega Megadrive again!'

17 Insanity is hereditary. We get it from our children.

Preachers on Parade

A fact that has escaped many preachers is that Christ did not say to his followers:

'Ye must be bored again.'

However, glazed eyes, slumped heads, dropped jaws, or a curious tendency to count the flecks on the old lady's coat in the next pew, are just a few of the hallmarks of the 'bored-again' Christian.

'Ye shall know them by the matchsticks propping up their eyelids.'

It is regrettable that many preachers do not take the sound advice about their sermons which is closer than they think — namely, the word: 'Pulp-it'.

One could attempt a useful definition of the art of the preacher, by adapting some words of W.H. Auden: A preacher is 'someone who talks in someone else's sleep.'

18 A minister was preaching in the chapel of a psychiatric hospital. In the middle of his sermon, one of the patients stood up and shouted: 'How long have we got to listen to this appalling rubbish?'

The minister turned to the consultant psychiatrist next to him and whispered nervously, 'Shall I stop speaking?'

'No, no, go ahead,' said the psychiatrist.

'But what if he interrupts again?' said the minister, not wanting to cause a scene.

'He won't, I can assure you,' said the psychiatrist. 'That man has only one lucid moment every seven years.'

19 A travelling preacher took his wife to one of his appointments. She was left on her own in the church and eventually sat down in a back pew. A steward came and chatted to her, not knowing who she was, but warmly welcomed her to the service. Afterwards, as she was on her way out, the steward whispered to her confidentially: 'Let me tell you, we don't get a duffer like this in the pulpit every Sunday.'

20 What's the difference between an audience and a congregation?

An audience listens.

21 An unrepentant parishioner accosted the vicar: 'Everything you say to me goes in one ear and comes out the other.'

'Of course,' smiled the vicar, 'there's nothing in between to stop it.'

22 'There was one passage at the end of your sermon which I found very helpful,' said an old lady to a young priest.

He was very flattered. 'Oh what was that?'

'Your passage from the pulpit into the vestry.'

23 The great nineteenth-century preacher, C.H. Spurgeon, conducted a 'masterclass' on sermons for his students. This was his advice:

'When you speak of Heaven, let your face light up, let it be irradiated by a heavenly gleam, let your eyes shine with reflected glory. But when you speak of Hell—your ordinary face will do.'

Years ago, at university, I occasionally went to lectures. Once, there was a visiting professor of literature who thumped the podium and warned us all: 'For goodness' sake remember, Ladies and Gentlemen, that a simplistic divergity is merely a pedagotistical device!' I've still no idea what he meant, but I did take his advice to remember this important fact.

At the same time, in the early seventies, there was a neat take-off of theological jargon going round. It went something like this:

> *'Jesus said to them: "Whom do you say that I am?" And they answered, "You are the eschatological manifestation of the ground of our being, the mystical essence of the divine kerygma."*
>
> *'And Jesus said: "Wot?" '*

24 Why did David prefer to be a door-keeper in the House of the Lord?

So he could stay outside while the sermon was being preached.

25 If the beard were all, the goat might preach. And frequently does.

26 A few hundred years ago, it was not uncommon for complacent clergymen to buy their weekly sermons. For a few pence, they could purchase a printed text and preach it as their own. Harrassed clergymen of today may regret the passing of this corrupt but somewhat imaginative solution to the Blank Mind on a Saturday Night Syndrome.

'Second-hand sermon salesmen' are an appealing concept:

'Sanctification. Excellent sermon. Superb theology. Hardly ever preached before.'

'Discerning the Will of God. Lovely line of argument. New trimmings and neat analogies. Only one careful preacher.'

Mind you, there are plenty of preachers out there already who can identify with the printer's error:

'Then the rector replied in a few appropriated words.'

27 One vicar I heard of was seriously caught out by a parishioner who came across the undeclared source of his sermon.

'You know, Vicar,' said the man with deep concern, 'they've got a cheek, haven't they? Taking that sermon you preached last Sunday and printing it—ten years ago.'

28 A visiting clergyman asked the church warden how long he should preach for. 'As long as you like,' said the church warden. 'Or as brief as *we* like.'

29 A verbose and extremely boring man said to the philosopher Plato, 'I hope I'm not boring you?' Plato smiled ingenuously. 'Oh no,' he said, 'I wasn't listening.'

30 A heckler called out to Herbert Silverwood, who was preaching in the open air: 'You're talking to yourself.'

'Never mind,' replied Silverwood, 'It always does me good to hear the gospel.'

31 A divinity lecturer was speaking at a famous university. On the stroke of twelve, students rudely began to snap their files shut and leave.

'Wait, Ladies and Gentlemen! Wait, please!' said the elderly professor commandingly. 'I still have a few more pearls to cast!'

32 A Strict and Particular Baptist preacher, reading from the Book of Acts about Philip baptising the Ethiopian eunuch, came to the line about them 'going down into the water' and interjected: 'Over the ankles—I concede no more!'

33 Bishop Sydney Smith devised the worst punishment imaginable. 'Sir,' he said to his adversary, 'you deserve to be preached to death by wild curates.'

34 After Canon David Watson had conducted his first three-hour Good Friday service, a woman came up to him. 'That was beautiful,' she sighed, 'and the bit I liked best was the silence.'

35 Cleaning out the pulpit, a caretaker found the typescript of last Sunday's sermon. He was intrigued to see that the vicar had pencilled notes to himself in the margin: 'Pause here for effect,' then further down, 'Wipe brow, sigh,' and half-way down the next page, 'Lift hands up to heaven.' After this there was a long, very involved piece of the sermon which the caretaker couldn't understand at all. Against this the vicar had written: 'Argument woolly and confused. Theology weak. Shout loudly and thump pulpit.'

36 A preacher in Cornwall puzzled his congregation by choosing the following text for his Harvest message: 'One of them that stood by drew his sword, and smote the servant of the high priest, and struck off his ear' (Mark 14 v 47).

When asked afterwards why he had not picked a more suitable text, he replied, 'No, this is a good one. Don't you see? First the blade and then the ear.'

(From the Major Chuckle column, edited by John Dixon, quoting The Church Times, *1971)*

37 A story is told of Dr Mahaffy, former provost of Trinity College, Dublin. When asked by a local clergyman how he had liked his sermon, Dr Mahaffy replied: 'It was like the peace and mercy of God.'

The clergyman was deeply flattered and wanted to know why he was making such a sublime comparison.

'Well,' said Dr Mahaffy, 'it was like the peace of God because it passed all understanding, and like his mercy because it showed every sign of enduring for ever.'

38 An absent-minded vicar was walking to a village church and preparing the sermon in his head. Wrapped in thought, he suddenly bumped into a cow. 'I beg your pardon, Madam,' he said—and then was extremely embarrassed to realise his mistake. Luckily, there were no witnesses to this incident. A mile further on, still preparing his sermon, he walked into the bishop's wife. Not to be taken in this time, he immediately shouted: 'Get out of my way, you silly old cow!'

39 One of the greatest advantages of religious broadcasting is that you can turn it off. Unfortunately, the average pulpit does not have a switch on its side. I sometimes fantasise about having a remote control device for making boring preachers vanish, or a button for fast-forwarding a repetitive train of thought:

'And so, dearly beloved brethren, I come to my main three points again, firstly thesplggffghwheeeeezzzrrr and so, in conclusion, let us say the grace together.'

40 The vicar stepped into the pulpit and opened up the Bible in front of him with a flourish.

'What does that mean, Daddy?' said the little boy in the front row.

'It means that he's going to tell us important things about the Bible.'

Then the vicar took out a sheaf of notes and laid them carefully on the lectern.

'What does that mean, Daddy?'

'That means he's going to explain all the things in the Bible story.'

Then the vicar took off his watch and put it on the side of the pulpit.

'What does that mean, Daddy?'

'That means absolutely nothing at all.'

Handle
With Prayer

I saw a cartoon recently which showed two doctors visiting a vicar who was laid up in hospital. 'Cheer up, Reverend,' they said, 'we'll have you back on your knees in no time.'

I can think of a few clergymen who'd rather be laid up in hospital. Prayer is a demanding activity, at the best of times, not least when faced with dilemmas like this:

———

41 Priest to Irish navvy in hospital:
'Michael, I'm going to pray that you will forgive O'Leary for throwing that brick at you.'

Michael:

'Perhaps you'd better wait till I'm better, father—and then pray for O'Leary.'

42 Everyone can sympathise with the desperate and doomed prayer of the schoolboy emerging from a geography exam: 'Dear God, please, *please* make Paris the capital of Turkey.'

43 David Watson was fond of quoting an MP on the subject of parliamentary prayer. According to the Right Honourable R. Witney, member for High Wycombe:

'The House of Commons begins its business with prayer each day. A chaplain follows the speaker into the House and turns round, looks at the MPs assembled, and prays fervently that God will have mercy on the nation.'

44 Such intercession is desperately needed if the spiritual life of one former MP is anything to go by. The Right Honourable John Ward composed this prayer in 1727:

'O Lord, thou knowest that I have nine houses in the city of London, and that I have lately purchased an estate in Essex. I beseech thee to preserve the two counties of Middlesex and Essex from fires and earthquakes. And, as I also have a mortgage in Hertfordshire, I beg thee also to have an eye on that county, and for the rest of the counties thou mayest deal with them as thou art pleased.'

(Quoted in The Methodist Church Ashfield Circuit Plan)

45 An indolent vicar of Bray
Let his lovely red roses decay;
His wife, more alert,
Bought a powerful squirt,
And said to her spouse, 'Let us spray.'

(From the Major Chuckle column,
edited by John Dixon)

46 The former West Indian cricketer, Sir Leary Constantine, was once the after-dinner speaker at a function in London. In introducing him, instead of saying, 'Pray silence for Sir Leary Constantine,' the Master of Ceremonies announced, 'Pray for the silence of Sir Leary Constantine.'

Rising slowly to his feet, Sir Leary said, 'Ladies and gentlemen, your prayers have been answered,' and momentarily sat down.

(Quoted in the Major Chuckle column, edited by
John Dixon, quoting the Rev. James A. Simpson,
Holy Wit, *G. Wright Publishers)*

47 A little girl's father was going to sea. She prayed: 'Dear Lord, please watch over my Daddy. And—' she added '—while you're at it, you'd better keep an eye on Mummy too.'

48 O God, for as much as without Thee
We are not able to doubt Thee,
Help us by Thy Grace
To convince the whole race
It knows nothing whatever about Thee.

(Ronald Knox)

49 'Why is it when I speak to God it's called "praying", but when God speaks to me they call it "paranoid schizophrenia"?'

(Graffiti)

50 A fly was looking up at a praying mantis. 'What are you doing?'

'I'm praying,' said the mantis.

'Don't be ridiculous,' said the fly, 'insects don't pray!'

The mantis swooped down and seized the fly in its claws, and the fly began: 'Our Father, which art in heaven, hallowed be thy name...'

51 A small boy, asked by his mother to pray for fine weather to make Granny's rheumatism better, came up with this memorable prayer: 'Oh Lord, please make it hot for Grandma!'

Filthy Lucre

What is the secret of happiness? One businessman put it very simply:

'The important thing is to be content with one's lot— provided it's a whole lot.'

———

52 When someone says, 'It's the principle of the thing, not the money'—it's the money.

(Kim Hubbard)

53 A Scottish visitor to the Holy Land was outraged at the cost of a boat trip on Galilee. He was told it would be the equivalent of £35. 'Do you realise,' he said, 'I can hire a boat for a week on Loch Lomond for that?'

'Ah, but sir,' the guide explained, 'these are the waters on which our Lord himself walked.'

'No wonder he walked,' said the Scotsman.

54 The story is told of Mark Twain attending a service for a charity in New York. Before the sermon, he placed a twenty-dollar bill on the pew ledge. After ten minutes had elapsed, he replaced it with a ten-dollar bill. After twenty minutes, he removed the ten-dollar bill. The preacher droned on for a long time. Finally, when the collection plate came round, Mark Twain *took out* a twenty-dollar bill.

55 A burglar was stumbling around in the darkness of a vicar's bedroom. The vicar stirred. 'Wh-who's there?'

'Don't move!' hissed the burglar, pushing a gun in his face, 'I'm hunting for your money.'

'Oh, well, turn the light on,' said the vicar, 'and I'll hunt with you.'

56 The offering had been taken in the tiny country church, but at the end of the service there was a special collection for missionary work. Most of the parishioners were poor but they gave generously. Finally, the bag came round to the lady of the manor. She turned away haughtily. 'I do *not* give money to missions.'

'Then take some out of the bag, your ladyship,' said the verger, 'this money is for the heathen.'

57 Two spiders lived in a church. One complained that he couldn't sleep because of the terrible thumping and banging.

'Where do you live?' said the other.

'Under the pulpit.'

'Oh,' said his friend, 'you'll have to come and live where I do––in the missionary box. There's total silence in there.'

58 Every Sunday a little boy went to church, tightly clutching his 10p for the collection. One Sunday, a guest came with his family. When the collection plate came near, the little boy whispered: 'Where's your 10p?'

'I haven't got one,' said the flustered guest.

'Quick—you take mine,' said the little boy magnanimously 'I'll get under the seat.'

59 One woman to another: 'I want my children to have all the things I couldn't afford—then I shall move in with them.'

60 A collector for Christian Aid was told by a householder, 'I'm sorry, I can't give anything, our dog ate the envelope you left.'

'That's all right,' replied the collector, 'I've got a spare envelope here.'

'That's no good,' said the householder quickly, 'he'd only eat that one too.'

(From the Major Chuckle column, edited by John Dixon, quoting Phil Mason, Christian Crackers, *Vol II, published by Norheimsund Books and Cards)*

61 Husband to wife in New York: 'Honey, if God had wanted us to have money, he would have made us TV evangelists.'

(From a Flying Fish postcard, Artpost, New York)

The Laughter Clinic

One of the most bizarre developments of recent times is the 'Laughter Clinic'—a place where people practise laughing at themselves, in order to deal more effectively with stress. A Christian equivalent might not be a bad idea: a healing centre which offers the 'laying on of jokes' for those who are in danger of taking themselves too seriously...

Ten years ago, I gave a seminar at the Greenbelt Festival with the title: 'How to be a fool for Christ without being a superspiritual idiot.' This is no easy task, as I discovered at the age of fifteen:

My friend Paul Burbridge (now Artistic Director of Riding Lights) and I were going through a very pious phase as teen-agers. We had missed a bus to an important church meeting— so we decided to kneel down by the side of the road, close our eyes and pray that God would send us another bus. As our eyes were shut, the bus went past. Someone later pointed out to us that this would never have happened if we had followed the advice in the Bible to 'watch and pray.'

I make no apologies for repeating this story, first published in Rolling in the Aisles, because it is one of my claims to expertise in the area of superspiritual idiocy. Some of the *material that follows in this chapter originated in the Greenbelt Seminar (later published in the magazine Ship of Fools) but I have added some more weird and wacky extremes.*

---

62 There is a church in Huthwaite, Nottinghamshire, which has a letter missing from a sign outside—it reads: 'Assemblies of od.' This might describe the people involved in the following incident:

63 Many years ago, a wise pastor I knew was approached by a young man who was convinced he was possessed by the Spirit of Cream Buns. Incredible though it sounds, the belief was genuine. He just couldn't stop eating cream buns and was convinced that this was a demonic craving. The pastor did not conduct an exorcism. (How would one go about such a thing? 'Oh Cream Cake come forth!' 'Depart from him, thou Chocolate Eclair!'?) My friend, a remarkable man of God, had a divinely inspired solution. He told the young man that his problem needed very special treatment. He should bend over and touch his toes. He did so. Then the pastor kicked him up the backside and said, 'That's for being such an idiot.'

64 This reminds me of my favourite lyric in a gospel song, which has the line: 'Drop kick me, Jesus, through the goalposts of life!'

This sheds an entirely new light on the idea of being 'instantly converted'.

65 Roger Royle recounted the following incident in his column 'The Royle Mail', for *Woman's Realm* (May 21 1988):

An open-air service was being held. 'At this particular location—I will not say where as that would be unfair to the many good and honest people who live in the area— there were a lot of people who, when they sang, liked to put their hands in the air. Seeing the people with their hands uplifted in prayer and joy was too much for some members of the community, whose fingers tended to be a little bit lighter than those raised in praise; so they seized upon the opportunity to pick the pockets of those whose minds were on a far higher plane—and whose pockets were unguarded. It ended in three arrests and others counting the cost of what they had lost.'

66 I am told the following incident occurred a few years ago in an English house church. I cannot verify it but, in some corners of God's Kingdom, fact is usually more bizarre than fiction. A small group were praying for a young man. They had gathered round in a circle, laid hands on him, and were desperately hoping that the Holy Spirit would fall on him and that the young man would duly speak in tongues. Perhaps he was resisting God. Perhaps there was some unconfessed sin. Perhaps they all lacked faith—because nothing happened whatsoever.

Still speaking English, the young man made his apologies and left, grateful to escape what felt more like a prayer beating than a prayer meeting. The zealous Christians prayed on fervently, convinced that he would soon start speaking in tongues, perhaps on his way home.

Meanwhile, the young man had discovered to his horror that his precious motorcycle had been stolen. Crying, stumbling, he rushed back into the prayer meeting and blurted incoherently:

'S-s-s-someone'sstolenmyKawasaki!'

At which all those in the prayer meeting shouted, 'Praise the Lord! Hallelujah!'

67 Strange how, when some people talk of gifts of the Spirit, they prefer the dramatic ones. They tell of receiving the gift of prophecy, of healing, or of speaking in tongues but never, somehow, the gift of administration. Not surprising, really. It doesn't sound very impressive to say:

'I was praying fervently the other night and, do you know, suddenly, amazingly, I started to type these letters!'

68 I've heard of a school in this country which teaches children 'Christian Education' in a very literal sense. If you walk in, you'll see on the wall posters illustrating the numbers one to ten. Not 'one cat', 'two dogs', 'three birds' and 'four cows'; but 'one Lord', 'two fishes', 'three days before the Resurrection', 'four gospels', 'five loaves', and so on.

Somewhere is the implication that ordinary things are not holy enough. 'All right, dogs, cats, cows and pigs, off you go! You're not spiritual enough. No grunting, unless it's in Hebrew, and no woofing unless it's theologically correct.'

But if you think this kind of 'Christian Education' is narrow, it's nothing compared to a little American book in my possession which glories in the title: *My Jesus Pocket Book of Nursery Rhymes*. Unsuitable traditional rhymes have been adapted for the Christian child. For example:

> Jack and Jill went up the hill
> To fetch some living water,
> Drank it down and saw they'd found
> Joy and life ever after.

Or there's this one:

> Wee Willie Winkie
> Runs through the town,
> Upstairs and downstairs
> In his nightgown.
> Peeping in the window,
> What does he see?

The children don't have time for Jesus,
They're watching TV.

Arguably, TV is a great deal more interesting than censored nursery rhymes which don't scan. However, there's no limit to the re-writing of our culture. Here's one of mine:

69 Humpty Dumpty sat on a wall,
Humpty Dumpty had a great fall,
This gave him the feeling
To seek Inner Healing,
And now he's no problems at all.

In fact, if you take this 'Christanising' principle to its logical conclusion, you can't go into a sweet shop with your children to buy ordinary sweets—you have to buy special Christian sweets for them: 'A quarter of Liquorice Allsouls please, and a packet of Evanjelly Tots.' Or what about, 'Milky Pray: the sweet you can eat during evensong'?

70 One of the sermon illustrations I remember most vividly from my childhood was about a soldier whose life was saved by the Bible in his breast pocket. A bullet went straight into the Bible, getting no further than about the Minor Prophets—which is a great deal further than many people get. However, the bullet failed to reach its destination and the man was saved. The moral was clear: the Word of God was a defence against the enemy and an instrument of salvation. This analogy worked perfectly well until, many years later, I stayed with a lady in the north of Scotland. She had on her mantlepiece a photo of her Uncle Willie, in First World War uniform, and next to it a copy of his bloodstained New Testament. It had been grazed by a bullet, which had cut a channel through the edge of the pages into his heart. This, I thought, is the penalty of reading only the New Testament. Conversely, what if the British army had all been supplied with Matthew Henry's commentaries? The Germans would have retreated in confusion...

71 I once attended a revivalist meeting at a Pentecostal church. The place was packed and there was an air of feverish anticipation. There were many choruses and a long preamble of prayer and praise. Then we were told, 'The Holy Spirit will be coming tonight!' I almost expected the speaker to continue, 'But unfortunately his train has been delayed.' However, the atmosphere heightened, emotions were keyed up. Something was going to happen: something incredible.

It did. There was a power cut, which seemed a little ironic in the circumstances.

72 Explaining the paradoxes of spiritual experience is sometimes very difficult. Only a few weeks ago, I heard of a healing meeting in Guildford—the speaker cancelled at the last minute because of ill-health.

73 A Christian book was an amazing success, despite false claims and outlandish promises. It was full of exaggerations and distortion: 'Amazing True Life Stories' which turned out to be amazing stories that had little connection to life or the truth. But in magazine adverts and on posters the message was proclaimed all over the country, which was effectively: 'Buy this book. It will change your life' (perhaps more correctly interpreted as 'Buy this book and the author can change his car'). On one of the posters, outside a Christian bookshop, it had a picture of the book with the caption: 'Over One Million Copies Sold!' Mindful of the fact that such a statistic might not be a recommendation of the book, but a condemnation of those who had bought it, someone had written in the corner:

'One million lemmings can't be wrong.'

74 There was a dry observation in a recent Sunday paper report of a healing rally:

'The evangelist shouted above the noise, "Those who need to be healed have sixty seconds to get on stage." The absence of a ramp for wheelchairs dealt nicely with the problem of producing any visible instant miracles.'

(Sunday Independent)

75 On more than one occasion my brother-in-law—a witty and straight-talking Nottinghamshire man—has brought the subject of religion firmly down to earth. One moment stands out for me. I told him about a faith healer I had met who taught that if a person is deaf all he has to do is 'stick his fingers in his ears and pray and he will be healed.' Paul thought about this for a moment and said: 'I pity anyone with piles.'

Since we have had recent election broadcasts on behalf of the Natural Law Party, which encourages 'Yogic flying', it is worth remembering that spiritual idiocy is not by any means an affliction unique to the fringes of Christianity. Some religions make it a fundamental requirement of their creed.

76 According to a report in the nineteen-seventies, 'Wealth seems to have materialised about the Majari Maharaj Ji (of the Divine Light Mission) in the most surprising places. When stopped at the US customs and asked what was in his baggage, the sage replied: "Dirty laundry". The ungodly officials, however, opened his bags and found £30,000 worth of jewellery. When questioned about the discrepancy in material reality, he was overheard to reply: "It's a miracle!" '

(Quoted in Really *magazine, Cambridge, 1973)*

77 A Surrey man applying for new National Health spectacles said his old ones had been dematerialised at a spiritualist seance.

(From a report in the Sunday Express*)*

78 The evening of clairvoyance on Tuesday, 4th December at 7pm has been cancelled owing to unforeseen circumstances.

(Notice in the East Kent Times*)*

79 Some cults and strange religious sects might do well to take on board Winston Churchill's main qualifications for being a politician: 'The ability to foretell what is going to happen tomorrow, next week, next month and next year—and the ability afterwards to explain why it didn't happen.'

80 My father, an ornithologist, has recorded and analysed on computer hundreds of different bird songs. Recently a man came to him with a curious request. He had been given my father's name as one of the few people in Britain who could analyse for him a strange trilling noise, which he and other colleagues had picked up on a tape-recorder at the dead of night in a cornfield.

They were 'crop circle watchers' and were convinced that they had heard the sound of a UFO or an alien life form. It had been picked up whilst they were silently meditating in a field.

My father produced a sonic graph of the unearthly sound. It turned out to be a grasshopper warbler, not from Mars but from Surrey. The poor bird was so disorientated, probably by the sight of humans in anoraks gathering pointlessly in a cornfield, that it was singing a strangulated version of its song at the dead of night.

Wisecracks

'Good things often come in small packages,' as they say, and a neat one-liner can say more than a whole script. I remember Mike Yarwood summing up the whole of the 1979 General Election with the words:

'The British do not like political jokes. This is because so many of them get elected.'

It is surprising how a complex subject like religious prejudice can be aptly expressed in seven words:

81 A man's best friend is his dogma.

———

Here are a few more wisecracks, ranging from the frivolous to the profound.

82 Bread might be the staff of life, but life isn't one long loaf.

83 We are the people our parents warned us about.
(Graffiti)

84 A Christian is a man who feels
Repentance on a Sunday
For what he did on Saturday
And is going to do on Monday.
(Thomas R.Y. Barra, 'The Christian')

85 A gossip is a person with a keen sense of rumour.

86 Any fool can criticise—and many of them do.

87 If you can keep your head when those about you are losing theirs—perhaps you've misunderstood the situation.

88 'Laugh,' they said, 'Life could be worse'. So I did, and it was.

89 A pessimist is a man who has to choose between two evils and chooses both.

90 Advice can often be had for nothing and is usually worth less.

91 As the Devil said to Noah: 'It's bound to clear up.'

92 Fools wander, wise men travel.

93 None goes so far as he who does not know whither he is going.

(*Oliver Cromwell*)

94 It is a wise man that has his after-thoughts first.

95 Early to rise and early to bed
Makes a man healthy and wealthy and dead.

(*James Thurber*)

96 It is better to say, 'This one thing I do,' than to say, 'These forty things I dabble in.'

97 We have just enough religion to make us hate, but not enough to make us love each other.

(*Jonathan Swift*)

98 To love the world for me's no chore
My problem is the man next door.

99 The least important fact about life is the score at half-time.

(James Brown)

100 Two men looked out from prison bars.
One saw mud, the other saw stars.

101 All men are equal—but it's what they're equal to that counts.

Clerical
Errors

A university friend and I had the habit of sending each other insulting letters. A competition developed to see who could produce the finest put-down, but judging from this classic reply, I think I lost:

———

102
13 November 1975

Dear Watts,

I acknowledge receipt of your recent (undated) letter.

With reference to your first sentence, 'Thank you for the latest installment of pedantic rubbish...', I should point out that instalment is spelt with one 'l' and not two,

Yours Sincerely,

P.A. Bolton.

It is no surprise that the author of this letter has subsequently had an extremely successful career in the civil service.

Fortunately for this section in the book, very few writers or printers have such a bureaucratic eye for errors.

103 Mrs Oakley wishes to thank the nurses and doctors for their kind cooperation in the loss of her husband.

(North Bucks Times)

104 A committee of ladies, with Mrs Griffiths leading the way, enthusiastically threw themselves into the tea.

(Devon paper)

105 The behaviour of many guests at wedding receptions is superbly conveyed by this local newspaper report:

'The bride sat down at the wedding table, surrounded by displays of red noses.'

John Dixon has sent me the following five items from his Major Chuckle column:

106 The following notice in a church newsletter could have been better expressed: 'Children are normally collected during the Offertory Hymn.'

107 Then there was the response to an equal opportunities ad, which read, 'I am replying to your advertisement for an organist and choirmaster, either lady or gentlemen. I have been both for many years.'

> *(Major Chuckle, quoting John Drew, 'Look at Life', in the Methodist Recorder)*

108 After a church organ had been repaired, a note was left on it which read, 'You can now change your combinations without taking your feet off the pedals.'

> *(Major Chuckle, quoting St Peter's Church Magazine, Woodmansterne)*

109 Another parish magazine reported: 'The sudden gust of wind took all who were at the ceremony completely by surprise. Hats were blown off and copies of the Vicar's speech and other rubbish were scattered over the site.'

(Major Chuckle, quoting Ninfield and Hove Parish News)

110 A report on a successful church appeal read as follows: 'The restoration of the church was completed by the re-surfacing of the driveway, when, to the applause of all who helped, the vicar and his wife rolled in the new gravel.'

(Major Chuckle, quoting Rosamund Essex in the Church Times)

---

111 We are most grateful to those who so kindly repaired the dilapidated hassocks for the church. Let us kneel on them.

(Wiltshire paper)

112 There was an unusual case of ancient tribal customs being revived in the Home Counties. The local paper referred to 'the couple exchanging their cows at a wedding.'

113 The vicar, the Rev C.O. Marston, reported an increased number of communicants during the year. He also stated that the death watch beetle had been confirmed in the church.

(Banbury Guardian)

114 Two printing errors offer revealing insights into the ministry. One described a country vicar as 'the local incumbrance for thirty years'.

115 Another dubbed the local minister as 'The Neverend Mr Smith'.

116 Reading the Bible aloud, with all the complicated words and names, can be one of the most stressful experiences. I remember when I was about seven struggling through a passage in the Gospels. It was family prayers and so there was always a strong possibility of some giggling from my brother, sister and myself. But this was serious. It was about the devil. The problem was that I pronounced his name 'Beezle-bub', and even the adults laughed.

117 I have no doubt that even the most self-controlled people laugh sometimes at mistakes in church because the incongruity is so overwhelming. It may seem irreverent to some, but I have a feeling that a church where no one ever smiles is more of a problem to God than the occasional outburst of people snorting and wimpering with laughter in the back pew. Peter Lawrence tells of an old parishioner called Daisy who read a line from the passion story like this:

'At the Ninth Hour Jesus cried with a loud voice, " 'Ello, 'ello"!'

118 There is also the well-known danger of turning several pages over at once. The famous examples are:

'Moses fell sick...and the lot fell upon Aaron.'

And:

'Judas went and hanged himself...go thou and do likewise.'

119 One has to admire the man who struggled so valiantly with the passage in Daniel which listed all the musical instruments to be played in worship of Nebuchadnezzar. Again and again, he came to the dreaded words, 'At the sound of the horn, pipe, lyre, trigon,' etc. and made a complete spaghetti bolognaise of it: 'the pipe, the lip, the popcorn, the tiger'. Eventually he just gave up and, when the list came up for the third time, he said simply: 'And the band played on.'

120 Most of the time, the laity can relax. It's the clergy who are often teetering on the edge of comprehension. One very nervous preacher began his address: 'I wish to say a few words before I begin.'

Presumably he was about to discuss the theory of relativity.

121 Another leant forward confidently and launched his address with:

'As I was sitting down there on my thought, a seat struck me.'

122 A gospel preacher was once engaged in a vivid retelling of the Prodigal Son story. He came to the scene in the pig-sty. This is how he described the young man's decision to return to his father:

'He took off his hat and threw it away. He took off his coat and threw it away. He took off his shirt and threw it away. Then at last he came to himself.'

123 But far more embarrassing than this, was the vicar who got carried away in his sermon on creation. 'Remember,' he declared to the packed church, 'that the same Creator who made the vast ocean made the glistening dewdrop, the Creator who made the mountain range made the flawless gemstone and'—he paused for effect, gathering inspiration from the flowers on the altar—'the same Creator who made me, made a perfect pansy.'

124 A famous preacher was the guest of an open-air festival of praise. He was telling the crowd of the faithful that Heaven will be a wonderful place. He concluded powerfully: 'We will all of us meet in a better land.' He then turned to the local organiser and said: 'I don't think I spoke for too long, did I?'

Unfortunately, the microphone was switched off too late. What the audience heard was: 'We will all of us meet in a better land. I don't think.'

125 When I went to give a talk at Lancaster University, I was met at the station by a man with a broad smile and an outstretched hand. 'Hello!' he roared, 'You *must* be Mr Stanley.'

It was hard to argue with such an authoritative tone. 'Oh, very well then,' I said, 'If you insist.'

He soon realised I was an impostor, when someone else came up to me and said, even more authoritatively, 'You must be Murray Watts!'

I've often thought, over the years, that I should have kept up the illusion of being Mr Stanley. My life might have turned out very differently. I could be living in the Bahamas by now, whilst Mr Stanley would be trying to explain himself yet again to his bank manager.

126 David Watson had a more memorable case of mistaken identity, when he was running a mission in Northampton. Whilst he was in the shopping mall, he was invited by a Christian to go to one of the meetings. 'I'm already going, as I'm somewhat involved,' David replied. 'Oh,' said the woman, 'are you part of David Watson?' 'I am David Watson.'

127 David was always telling stories at his own expense. One introduction he was given went like this: 'Some of you have heard David Watson before and some of you haven't. Those of you who haven't will be looking forward eagerly to hearing from him.'

(Told by Professor John Ferguson)

128 A minister once preached on the text, 'Naaman was a commander of the Syrian army, *but* he was a leper.'

As the sermon was well received he decided to use it again during an American exchange. Unfortunately, he did not realise that Americans use the word 'butt' to refer to a person's posterior. The three points of his sermon were:

'Every one of us has a but.'

'It is easy to see other people's buts.'

'It is difficult to see your own but.'

(From the Major Chuckle column, edited by John Dixon, quoting Rev. James A. Simpson, Holy Wit, G. Wright Publishers)

129 A Christmas party was being held in the church hall. Things were going a bit slowly and the children looked bored. The new minister decided to rescue the day. He organised adults and children into an impromptu game with the reward of a box of chocolates. The object was to make the ugliest face in the world. He gave the prize to one person who had been doing a great deal to help with the party and who, he felt, needed encouraging.

'Thank you very much, vicar,' said the quiet spinster, 'but I wasn't playing.'

130 An absent-minded vicar declared loudly: 'I publish the banns of marriage between—' then promptly forgot the names of the couple. 'Between...' he continued hopefully, but it was no good. He fumbled around for the register of names which was normally kept under his chair. The verger whispered to him, 'It's between the cushion and the seat.'

The vicar stood up confidently: 'I publish the banns of marriage between the cushion and the seat.'

Priceless
Pearls

At a parents' evening recently, I looked through my six-year-old son's workbook. He had drawn a picture of a knight on horseback. Underneath he had carefully inscribed: 'This is a picture of me as a nit'.

My wife commented drily, 'Like father, like son.'

Here are some more howlers, taken from generations of schoolchildren.

---

131 A certain man drew his bow at a venture but missed the venture and hit Ahab.

132 An epistle is the wife of an apostle.

133 An evangelist is one who brings the gossip.

134 Joseph had a goat of many colours, but it got him out of the pit all right.

135 In the book of Job, Satan is no ordinary devil. He is the Attorney-General.

136 Q. Who said: 'What mean ye by these stones?'
A. It was said by Goliath to David.

137 He was dressed in the garbage of a monk.

138 A horse divided against itself cannot stand.

139 You can tell a Gothic Cathedral by its flying buttocks.

140 The crusades were fought in plasticine.

141 You shall not admit adultery.

142 Whenever David played to Saul, the latter kept a javelin handy.

143 Elijah was known as the Fishbite. No one knows why.

144 Peter warmed his hands at a damsel.

145 Jesus healed ten leopards and the one that lost his spots came back to thank him.

146 It is hard for a man with a camel in his eye to walk into a needle as to the man to give up his wealth.

147 Q. What is the meaning of 'Ave Domine'?
A. Lord, I am a bird.

148 Sins of omission are those we have forgotten to commit.

149 Mary Magdalene returned to the womb but found it empty.

150 Wild beasts used to roam at will in England, but now they are only found in theological gardens.

151 Thomas à Becket met Henry on the altar steps and said: 'What ho, King!' Henry massacred him severely.

152 A casserole is a garment chiefly worn by curates.

153 Solomon had 300 wives and 700 porcupines.

154 God tired Abraham.

155 A deacon is a mass of inflammable material placed in a prominent position to warn the people.

156

Q. Who said: 'See that thou fall not out by the way'?

A. Elisha to Elijah when the latter went up to heaven in a chariot.

157

Every year the Pope sent missionaries to invert the Chinese.

158

A pessimist is a man who is never happy unless he is miserable. Even then he isn't happy.

159

Noah was the man who danced before the ark, but he first sent the bird away.

160

The Sadducees did not believe in spirits, but the Publicans did.

161 A sackbut is a large measure of wine, much favoured in biblical times.

162 When the dinner bell went all the monks would crow outside the refectory.

163 The Black Hole of Calcutta was a small dark prison with ninety men and only one widow in it. In the morning all the men were dead.

164 Salome took off all her clothes and danced before Harrods.

165 Eliza came before the king wrapped in a camel's hair and said: 'Behold me, I am Eliza the Tit-bit.'

166 An octopus is a person who hopes for the best.

167 B.C.   Before Christ
A.D.   After the Devil

168 After I had been in the Scouts a month, I was publicly unrolled.

169 The prevailing religion in England is hypocrisy.

170 The Prodigal Son was a bit of a swine, but not near his father.

Original Sins

If St Paul had been alive today, he might have used the supermarket trolley as his analogy for human nature: 'When I push it forward, it swerves to the left. When I pull it backwards, it swerves to the right. It only ever goes straight down the aisle when I want to turn a corner.'

———

171 Much of contemporary morality could be summed up in the motto: 'Two wrongs don't make a right—so why not try three?'

172 The perversity of human nature is well summed up by Thomas Nashe:
   'A great many more people would want to go to church if there were a law against it.'

173 As for obeying the Ten Commandments, G.K. Chesterton's comment on the personal morality of Bertrand Russell would go for many of us:

'He treated the Ten Commandments like one of those exam papers, which have at the top: "Not more than six of these should be attempted." '

174 One zealous preacher was thundering away on the subject of Original Sin and Falling from Grace. It was a powerful theological diatribe, inspiring, challenging and incomprehensible. An old lady listened to him nervously, nodding her head, only understanding a few words here and there.

He leant forward from the pulpit: 'Madam—do *you* believe in the doctrine of Falling from Grace?'

'I believe it,' she said, nodding her head furiously, 'and praise God, I practise it!'

175 Notice in a works office: 'All requests for leave of absence on account of bad colds, headaches, sick relatives, funerals, weddings...must be handed to the Head of the Department before 10 am on the morning of the match.'

176 A very pious woman was delighted to find that her new neighbours were Christians. However, her opinion of them plummeted when she found a message on her door one Sunday: 'Could we borrow your lawnmower please?'

'It's disgusting,' she said, 'mowing the lawn on a Sunday. Have they no respect for the Lord's Day? It really is shameful!' She turned to her husband. 'Go and tell them we haven't got a lawnmower.'

177 A man was being baptised in a remote village, high in the mountains. Before his conversion he had been an outrageous liar, and the villagers were sceptical of this sudden change of heart. The missionary doused him in the freezing waters of a mountain river and the man emerged shivering.

'Is it cold?' asked the missionary, anxiously.

'No, it's fine,' said the man.

'Duck him again, Pastor,' shouted a villager, 'he's still a liar!'

178 A leading member of the Lord's Day Observance Society was secretly playing a round of golf on a Sunday. It was a remote country club and no one saw him—except the angel on duty in heaven.

'Lord,' said the angel, 'surely this man should be punished for his hypocrisy?'

'Good idea,' said the Lord. He stretched out his right hand in heaven and, down on earth, an extraordinary miracle happened: the man teed off for the final and most difficult hole; his ball whizzed an impossible distance through the air, curving past a clump of trees and suddenly gaining height over a bunker. At last, to the man's astonishment, it plopped straight into the eighteenth hole.

'But Lord,' protested the angel, deeply shocked, 'that's hardly a punishment.'

'Oh, it is,' said the Lord, laughing softly. 'Who can he *tell*?'

179 A vicar on a bus, noticing a man who was very much the worse for wear, summoned the conductor: 'Are drunks allowed on this bus?'

'No, sir,' whispered the conductor, 'but if you sit down and keep quiet, no one will notice you.'

180 A man was explaining to his son how ethics were vital to everyday living.

'The other day a friend paid me back a loan with a new ten-pound note. As he was leaving, I discovered he'd given me two notes stuck together. At once a question of ethics arose: Should I tell the wife?'

(From the Major Chuckle column, edited by John Dixon, quoting from Quotes and Anecdotes, *by Anthony P. Castle, published by Kevin Mayhew Ltd)*

181

Judge: Why didn't you plead guilty at the start and save us a lot of time?

Prisoner: I thought I was innocent but that was before I had heard the evidence against me.

(Quoted by David Watson)

182

Woman to policeman: Arrest that man! He just came up to me and whispered that I was the most gorgeous creature he'd ever seen.

Policeman: What shall I arrest him for, Madam? Drunkenness or insanity?

183 The nineteen-year-old driver had his red Fiat covered in brash stickers and loaded with fluffy dice and trinkets. He always drove with one elbow leaning out of the window, quadraphonic stereo blaring down the street. On his dashboard, a St Christopher medallion had pride of place amongst all the lucky charms.

Hurtling down the motorway one day, at ninety miles an hour, he heard a voice crackling from his radio.

'St Christopher speaking. You're on your own now. Over.'

184 A century ago, a Jesuit missionary returned to the South Sea Islands to discover that the whole tribe had reverted to cannibalism. He found one of his most promising converts, a young altar boy, and shook him: 'Surely you didn't take part in the feast, did you?'

The boy was horrified. 'What, eat human flesh?!' The priest breathed a sigh of relief. 'How could I possibly do that, Father? It was a Friday.'

185 A bishop was staying with a very strict Christian. Early one evening, he tactfully withdrew to the vegetable patch at the end of the garden in order to light his pipe secretly—but the pious Christian happened to be in the garden shed. He flung open the window suddenly and shouted: 'You are burning incense to the devil!'

'I didn't realise you were so close,' said the bishop.

186 A clergyman had travelled a long way to speak at evensong in the village church. There was a reception committee waiting for him in the church hall, and one of the sidesmen offered him a glass of whisky.

'No, thank you,' said the clergyman emphatically, 'I refuse for three reasons: first, because I'm chairman of the Temperance Society, second because I'm just going into church, and third, because I've just had one.'

For Better
or For Worse

Some people hope for a 'marriage made in heaven'—but for most the relationship is rather more earth-bound.

187

| Young woman: | I want to marry a man who is rich, handsome and intelligent! |
| Counsellor: | So you're really looking for three husbands. |

188

First Woman:	I fell in love with my husband because I thought he was like a Greek god.
Second Woman:	Did he turn out to be one?
First Woman:	Yes. Bacchus.

189 The man murmured sweetly to his wife: 'You have the face of a saint,' then whispered in her ear, 'a Saint Bernard.'

190 A lady took her nephew to a wedding. The usher was directing the guests, friends and relatives of the bride to the left and the groom's family to the right.

'Which side are you on?' he asked.

Before she could answer, her nephew piped up enthusiastically, 'Oh, is there going to be a fight?'

(From the Major Chuckle column, edited by John Dixon, quoting a letter to Woman's Realm *magazine from Mrs C. Adamson)*

191 First Man: I proposed to a girl and would have married her if it hadn't been for something she said.

Second Man: What was that?

First Man: 'No.'

192 Two old friends met. 'How's your husband?' said one.

Her pious friend smiled complacently: 'Oh, he's an *angel*!'

'You're lucky,' said the other. 'Mine's still alive.'

193 'If my wife lived in India, she'd be sacred.'
(*Graffiti*)

194 A woman rushed into a psychiatric hospital and asked: 'Have any of your patients escaped?'

The doctors were puzzled. 'Not as far as we know—why?'

'Because someone's run off with my husband.'

195 A man was knocked over by a car. The driver leapt out and knelt by the figure lying in the road. Thinking he was seriously injured, the driver asked desperately, 'Have you a wife?'

'No,' the man groaned, 'up to now this is the worst thing that has ever happened to me.'

196 An arrogant Yuppie was talking to his father, a quietly spoken and wise old man.

'I feel it would be stupid of me to marry a girl who is intellectually my inferior,' said the son.

'Worse than stupid, my boy,' said his father, 'it would be impossible.'

197 Women who want to be equal to men lack ambition.

(Graffiti)

198 A man went to a psychiatrist, wearing a french horn strapped to his head, a bunch of bananas round his neck, a shirt made of chicken wire, a television aerial sticking out of his ear, and a couple of dead fish strapped to each foot.

'Doctor,' he said, 'I must talk to you about my wife.'

199 A Christian minister sent a Telemessage to his god-daughter for her wedding day. The biblical reference was 1 John 4:18. This reads: 'There is no fear in love; but perfect love casts out fear.'

Unfortunately, the telephonist left out the 1—making it a reference to John's Gospel. The bride was horrified to receive the message, read out in public: 'The man whom you now have is not your husband.'

200 The Reverend Peter Lawrence has sent me one of the finest 'Freudian slips' of any church service. He writes:

'In the wedding season there may be many names to be read out in the Sunday services, asking if anyone objects. It is easy to become a little absent-minded in such circumstances.

'A friend of mine found this happening to him and inadvertently said,

' "If any of you know cause, or just impediment, why these two persons should not be *joyfully loined* together, ye are to declare it."

'There were some present who felt the new wording was an improvement.'

201 The new curate, a handsome young bachelor, flirted outrageously with the ladies in the parish. He was surrounded by so many ardent admirers and created so much emotional havoc, that the vicar was at his wits' end. There were rumours of indiscretions, jealousies and rivalries. Finally, the vicar decided the curate would have to go. He called the man into his office and confronted him with the problem of all his lovesick admirers.

The curate shrugged his shoulders. 'There's safety in numbers,' he said.

'The only safety for you,' replied the vicar firmly, 'is in Exodus.'

202

First woman:	My husband knows his place. He has never spoken a harsh word to me in his life.
Second woman:	What a Christian gentleman he must be!
First woman:	Not Christian, so much as cautious.

203

| She: | There was something about you that I used to like once upon a time. |
| He: | Yes! But since we've been married, you've spent it all. |

204 Women like the simple things in life—men.

205 What is the penalty for bigamy?
Two mothers-in-law.

206 A girl came from a very strict religious background. One day, she came crying to her mother: 'I can't marry Julian after all—I've discovered he doesn't believe in Hell!'

'Don't worry,' thundered her mother, 'Get married—and I'll convince him of the existence of Hell!'

The Funny Side of Faith

I was once acting in a street-theatre play outside St. Nicholas'
Church in Durham. We were wearing red noses and clown
suits, old top hats and tails, long grey beards and huge plastic
ears—in other words, we were obviously normal Christians
engaged in a church mission. As we were dramatising one of
the parables of Jesus, Richard Mapletoft, one of the craziest
actors on our team, spotted the former Archbishop of Canterb-
ury, Lord Ramsay, walking slowly past. Taking off his plastic
ears, Richard approached him smiling. Lord Ramsay walked
on. Richard attempted to hand him a leaflet, explaining what
we were doing. Lord Ramsay quickened his pace. Richard
was left behind, but I spotted the ancient Archbishop too. Not
knowing that Lord Ramsay was now deliberately giving us a
wide berth, I decided to run up and say 'hello'. I had always
admired him very much and thought, mistakenly, that he
would like to hear about a group of young people reviving the
ancient art of the mystery plays in Durham. I should add that I
was not wearing any funny costume at the time, but was subtly
disguised as a sensible person, wearing a suit and tie. How-
ever, Lord Ramsay could see through this. He could tell that I
was clearly a sad and deranged individual who, in a few

minutes' time, would stop the religious chat and ask him for the price of a cup of tea. He started to move away very briskly indeed, without uttering a word. Realising that he thought I was barking mad, I walked back a little crestfallen and joined the street theatre show. What I didn't know at the time was that I was conducting the mission for the future Archbishop of Canterbury, George Carey, then vicar of St. Nicholas. I have often wondered what that made him, by association. Clearly a dangerous lunatic.

---

207 One event in the Christian calendar which is missing from modern times is the 'Feast of Fools'. In medieval England, a day was set aside when the laity took a holiday from their religious observances. The order of the establishment was reversed and a feckless young apprentice declared 'Abbot of Unreason' or 'Lord of Misrule'. Our April Fools day is a pale shadow of this tradition—but, on the other hand, we do have 365 days of folly provided by the government these days. Perhaps there should be one day in the year when politicians behave sensibly: a 'Feast of Wisdom', 'April Sages Day'.

Folly, as St. Paul brilliantly demonstrates in II Corinthians, is really a matter of perspective. Those who are most in need of wisdom are often the last to recognise it...

208 A Christian lady was boasting about her son.

'I have the most wonderful son in the world,' she said, deeply emotional, 'he visits me every Sunday after church. And do you know what he does? He waters the garden. Then he goes to evensong and he comes back, and he cleans the grate and he lights the fire. And then he goes home and he rings me up to see if I'm all right. Then each day he goes to work and, do you know, he rings me up at lunchtime to see if I'm happy. If ever he has a problem, he asks me to pray for him. If ever he wants to take a girl out, he brings a photo round and asks my opinion. Then every Friday he goes to see a psychiatrist and he talks to him for a whole hour. And do you know what he talks about?' She beamed with pride. 'He talks all about me.'

The story above suggests another annual event for the calendar: 'Smothering Sunday'.

Looking at our society and our families, it's surprising how many of us are sane ... or are we?

209 My doctor says I'm schizophrenic, but I don't believe him and neither do I.

(Graffiti)

210 A behavioural psychologist left a chimp in a room with toys and machines, and then looked through the spyhole to see what the chimp was doing. In fact, the chimp was also looking through the spyhole to see what the psychologist was doing.

(David Watson, from a story told by David Pawson)

I used to think that the main cause of stress in the world was all the books on the main causes of stress in the world. However, I added to the problem recently by writing another one. The ironies were overwhelming at the time. I was continually rushing to meet deadlines for the BBC publication. I could see the newspaper reports:

> *'Stress Author crashes car into BBC reception, staggers up steps to editor's office and collapses from coronary, trying to deliver manuscript on time.'*

The futility of rushing everywhere is aptly summed up by the following true incident:

211 Two trains, the 6.30 and 6.38 were about to leave a London station for Bishop's Stortford, from opposite platforms. Both guards assured respective passengers that the *other* train would leave first. As a result, both trains emptied simultaneously, and the passengers collided on the bridge connecting the two plat-forms. This was a good vantage point from which they could see both trains leaving the station—empty.

212 A young city businessman was rushing for a train on the Piccadilly Line. He stuck his foot in the door and it slid open again—but the carriage was jam-packed with people. Undeterred, he pushed up to an elderly clergyman who was hanging on for dear life.

'Excuse me,' said the arrogant young executive, 'but is there any room in this *Noah's Ark?*'

'Just about,' said the clergyman, 'everyone's here except the ass. Come on in.'

213 The twentieth century has been plagued with the notion of progress—meaning 'to keep blundering straight on regardless of the con-sequences.' The idea of changing course when lost has been slow to catch on. The illusion of progress is well illustrated by a favourite story of David Watson's:

A pilot, flying a 747 to New York, gave out this announcement:

'Ladies and Gentlemen, I've got some bad news and some good news for you. First, the bad news. I'm afraid we're completely lost. Now the good news. We're making good time.'

(Told by Peter Rogers at St Aldate's, Oxford)

214 An advertising company was recently commissioned to suggest ways of attracting candidates for the ministry. One of the copywriters came up with the line:

'Join the Christian ministry. The pay's terrible but the pension's out of this world.'

215 There have been some good adverts outside churches recently. This is one of the best:

'Go to church this Sunday—avoid the Christmas rush.'

216 My personal favourite is:

'Don't let anxiety kill you—allow the church to help.'

217 This is closely rivalled by:

'Be a missionary—give cannibals a taste of Christianity.'

218 Full marks to the vicar who held up a basket of groceries at the church harvest auction and said:

'There's a tin of prunes in this one. Buy it and be a regular church attender.'

219 One Christian bookshop, over forty years ago, led the way in advertising with this sign:

Holy Scripture, Writ Divine
Leather bound, at One and Nine,
Satan trembles when he sees
Bibles sold as cheap as these.

220 However, there is one problem with adverts, especially those outside churches. They attract the dreaded graffiti artist.

There was a notice outside a church: 'Tired of sin and longing for a rest?'

To which someone had added: 'If not, 'phone Grassmeer 63842.'

221 Two clergymen on a walking tour had lost their way. They arrived at a farm and were offered hospitality. The farmer provided two of his very best chickens, which his wife roasted. The clergymen ate their fill and retired to bed gratefully. In the morning, they were woken early by the cockerel crowing loudly.

Coming down to breakfast, one of the clergymen commented: 'He seems very pleased with himself.'

'So he should be,' said the farmer, 'two of his sons entered the ministry last night.'

222 Young men shall see visions
Old men shall dream dreams
But this won't make any difference because the middle-aged will still run the churches.

223 'Do not quarrel with an angry person, but give him a soft answer. It is commanded by Holy Writ and, furthermore, it makes him madder than anything else you could say.'

(*Sanderstead Church News, c.1950*)

224 We talk of the Amplified Bible, the Annotated Bible, the Authorised Version, the New International Version. Perhaps there should be a Sanitised Bible, with specially emended texts for the complacent Christian:

'Lord, here am I, send him.'

225 In the wake of controversy about Anglican bishops and belief, I was commissioned by Central Television to make an April Fool's Day documentary. It was directed by Michael Ruggins and featured members of Riding Lights Theatre Company, but was transmitted as part of a genuine documentary series called 'Encounter'. The film purported to be a visit to the 'Worldwide Anglican Renewal Project' (W.A.R.P.). This was a centre which offered therapy to clergymen who were in danger of regaining their faith. It was staggering how many people thought that the documentary was for real. At one point, we interviewed a clergyman who was 'guilty about still believing in the Bible' and wished to remain anonymous. We filmed him in silhouette, rather like an addict or a criminal. This was his confession, given in a hoarse whisper to the camera:

I am an Anglican minister. I was ordained twenty years ago. Ever since then, I have been troubled by my certainties. I started by believing that the Bible was a reliable record of events and then I couldn't stop. First, it was the miracles. Then, it was the Resurrection. It was terrible. I became increasingly convinced that it had actually happened. My bishop was very worried about me. He told me to take a holiday, but I spent the whole time in prayer. I felt I had let him down. He was very understanding, but told me to keep away from religious broadcasting. I tried questioning everything. I looked at two sides of every issue, I spoke in endless qualifications, I leant how to waffle, but it was all a pathetic sham! My congregation could see through it all. They knew that I believed. The bishop summoned me for a last warning. He told me to start losing my faith or get out of the church.

At one point in W.A.R.P. we showed an experiment in liturgy—a church service with rewritten hymns and prayers:

'Our Father, who may or may not be in Heaven, hallowed be your name, assuming there is someone up there, your kingdom come, your will be done, in a manner of speaking...'

But we went on to claim that a far more ambitious project was in hand:

226 'There is a new liturgical committee working for the Anglican church. They are seeking to align the church with the needs of the modern world and have therefore come up with a special 'Unconfirmation Service'. Candidates for Unconfirmation will kneel and express their lack of faith. The bishop will then lay hands on them and sympathise.'

The programme attracted a fascinating response, some people ringing the switchboard whilst the film was still on the air, to complain about this sinister project, others writing enthusiastically and begging for the spoof documentary to be repeated. As far as I know, only one bishop complained, which probably means that the vast majority of bishops have a great sense of humour—or, on the other hand, don't watch religious broadcasting, which may well amount to the same thing.

Here is a final extract, an 'opinion poll' we claimed to have taken:

'In a recent poll, Anglican bishops were asked if they felt that bishops suffered unfairly from being caricatured on television:

'77% said, "It depends what you mean by caricature."

'22% said, "It depends what you mean by unfairly."

'1% said, "It depends what you mean by bishop." '

227 After making W.A.R.P., Riding Lights considered other ideas for spoof documentaries. Here are the notes for one idea, which we never made, but has considerable potential:

'Suggestion: A deeply compassionate documentary about the problem of being a normal family.

'A "Forty Minutes/First Tuesday" style documentary, looking at the extraordinary case of Britain's normal families. Commentary: "Louisa is seven and has been read a bedtime story ever since she was two. Although young, she is distressingly aware of how much her parents love each other. Gradually, she has come to accept that they have no intention of leaving each other. This happiness in the home has alienated Louisa from her schoolfriends, all of whom come from the traditional broken home."

'The shock investigation reveals genuine love, compassion and fidelity in many homes. The documentary could end with an appeal:

' "Louisa has suffered happiness for too long. If you fancy a spot on the side and think you could run off with her Mummy or Daddy, then write to, 'The Breaking Up Homes Appeal', XYZ TV, London. Help Louisa to be like other children." '

228 One of the earliest satirists in the history of the world was the prophet Isaiah. He was surrounded by peoples who fervently believed in blocks of wood. This is how he put it:

> The carpenter cuts down a tree.... Then it becomes fuel for a man; he takes a part of it and warms himself, he kindles a fire and breaks bakes bread; also he makes a god and worships it, he makes it a graven image and falls down before it. Half of it he burns in the fire; over the half he eats flesh, he roasts meat and is satisfied; also he warms himself and says, 'Aha, I am warm, I have seen the fire!' And the rest of it, he makes into a god, his idol; and falls down to it and worships it; he prays to it and says, 'Deliver me, for thou art my God!'
> *(Isaiah 44:15-17, Revised Standard Version)*

Isaiah's end of term report probably read: 'This prophet should go far—and the further the better.' Tradition says that he ended his life in martyrdom. I sometimes wonder what Isaiah would have to say today about false worship—bowing down before cars, televisions, pop videos...or famous personalities at Christian conferences.

229 An Irish priest was asked: 'What's the difference between Cherubim and Seraphim?'
'Well, now,' he paused, 'there was a difference between them a long time ago, but surely to God they've made it up now?'

230 Q. Why is a Catholic priest like a bus conductor?
A. They both ring bells, take money, and tell people where to get off.

231 Times have changed in Wales since the days of the great revivals. Someone asked a young Welshman if he were 'church or chapel?'
'I don't really know,' he said, after long deliberation, 'but I suppose it's the church I avoid going to.'

232 One bishop's wife I knew handled an awkward situation at a tea-party with superb diplomacy. A foreign bishop was on his first visit to Britain. On the table before him were plates of cucumber sandwiches, small sausage rolls, vol-au-vents, and a number of cakes—including a large round sponge-cake. The cake had a knife beside it and was waiting to be cut into slices. However, the visiting bishop did not stand upon ceremony. Never having seen a sponge-cake before, he decided to help himself in a somewhat unconventional manner. He peeled off the whole top of the cake. Seeing him about to sink his teeth into the huge round disc, the English bishop's wife leant over and said, 'Oh, bishop, you won't get any *cream* that way.' She retrieved the top, deftly reconstructed the cake and proceeded to cut it into small slices.

233 Such culture clashes work both ways. I remember an upper-class English lady, provided with a bowl of passion fruit salad from Africa, desperately and methodically easing out every little black pip and laying them round the edges of her plate. The meal lasted for a very long time.

234 Then there was the coolness of the hostess who was faced with a twentieth-century descendant of Friar Tuck at one of her 'at homes'. As the clergyman stashed away the grub at a furious rate, she turned to her husband.

'Oh, Rodney,' she drawled, 'do look after the Rector—he's helping himself to *everything*.'

235 Many years ago, *Newsweek* published a list of modern euphemisms. They included:

Peacekeeper (nuclear missile)
Selected Out (you failed)
Negative Economic Growth (recession)
Terminal Living (dying)
Negative disassembly (explosion)

On contemporary morality, one could add:

Valuable Experience (an indefinite number of mistakes)
'Adult' movie (childish self-indulgence)
I did it my way (I'm an egotist and I'm proud of it)
I have no regrets (I've succeeded in stifling my conscience altogether).

236 Many Christians are addicted to euphemisms or jargon, and develop a kind of 'churchspeak'. An example of this was when David Watson was very ill. Someone was told on the 'phone that David had 'gone home'—meaning that he had returned to London. However, the rumour spread like wildfire that he had died and was now in heaven. David loved this story, reminiscent of Mark Twain's obituary, which appeared while he was still alive—'Reports of my death have been greatly exaggerated.'

237 Perhaps a kind of 'foreign language phrase book' is needed in the church to help us decipher the real meaning of many of our statements.

I suggest the following:

'The Lord's been teaching me a lot recently.' (I've been going through black despair.)

'We've really had to work out our relationship.' (I hate his guts.)

'The Lord led me to challenge her.' (I slagged her off to her face.)

'I handed it over to God.' (I lost control of the situation.)

238 At a cathedral service for laundry workers, the opening hymn was 'O for a faith that will not shrink,' to the tune 'Lux Benigna'. This was followed by 'What can wash away my stains,' to the tune

'Eventide'. The climax of the service was the hymn, 'All things bright and beautiful'.

239 Children often mishear prayers and hymns which they cannot read. My brother-in-law, at the age of four, wanted to know why he always had to pray for mice. He had been reciting the children's prayer, 'Pity my simplicity' as 'Pity mice implicitly'.

Then there was the child who wanted to know why God was called Harold—'Harold be thy name'—or the little girl puzzling over a hymn to a nineteenth-century prime minister: 'Letters with a Gladstone mind.'

An animal-loving child enjoyed the reference to a baby bear, in the lines: 'Can a woman's tender care/Cease towards the child she-bear'; and, of course, numerous children have been extremely fond of 'Gladly, the cross-eyed bear'.

240 As a child, I was even more fascinated by the names of hymn-writers than their lyrics. I would murmur them to myself, over and over again, imagining a long list of bizarre and exotic characters.

I would dream up adventures for them. There was the deadly Charles Coffin, the wicked J.M.C. Crum and the bumbling E.H. Plumptre. There was the bizarre Augustus

Montague Toplady and the terrifying Count Nicolas Ludwig von Zinzendorf—clearly from Transylvania. I went through the whole hymn book turning many saintly and famous Christians into villains.

Some names, however, immediately suggested themselves as heroic: there was the gallant Folliott Sandford Pierpoint and Horatius Bonar, clearly men who would know how to deal with criminals like Joseph Medlicott Scriven and the arch-fiend, Theodulph of Orleans.

Alongside these characters, in an epic drama forming in my mind, there were minor figures like the mysterious Anon, Traditional and Compiled. Sometimes hymn-writers were referred to as being 'altered' or, even more painfully, 'abridged'. There were the unfortunate cases of people who had verse six omitted.

Sadly, I have not grown up and become a mature Christian, because only the other day—on seeing the name F. Pratt Green in the hymn book—I could hear the conversation in my head:

Vicar: I say, was that Pratt Green in the front pew this morning?

Curate: No, it's just the way the light shines off the stained-glass windows.

The Twinkling
of an Eye

241 Some awkward misunderstandings arose when the first 'Body Shop' was opened in 1976, in Brighton—right next to a funeral parlour.

Death is certainly a confusing idea. My five-year-old son was thinking anxiously about death and nothing I could say to him offered a satisfactory explanation.

'What happens when you die?' he wanted to know.

'You go to heaven,' I said.

'Before that,' he said, irritated at my failure to grasp the simplest concept.

'Er...well, you go to sleep and sort of—'

A thought flashed into his mind: 'I know! What if you just go flying through the sky, screaming 'WHERE'S MY BODY?? WHERE'S MY BODY??' The image remained with me for a long time afterwards.

I lay in bed that night imagining a conversation between a seagull and a ghost:

137

Ghost: *You didn't see a body go past here, did you?*
Seagull: *Whose body?*
Ghost: *Mine, actually.*
Seagull: *Mmmm...did it have a beard and glasses?*
Ghost: *Yup, that's the one.*
Seagull: *I think it went over the North Pole.*
Ghost: *(flying off) Aaaaaah...where's my bodeeeeee....*

242 Death is only a state of mind.
Only it doesn't leave you much time to think about anything else.

(Graffiti)

243 Beneath this smooth stone by the bone of his bone
   Sleeps Master John Gill;
  By lies when alive this attorney did thrive,
   And now that he's dead he lies still.

(Anon)

 244 Mary Anne has gone to rest
Safe at last on Abraham's breast,
Which may be good for Mary Anne
But is certainly rough on Abraham.

245 A zealous locksmith died of late
And did arrive at heaven's gate.
He stood without and would not knock,
Because he meant to pick the lock.

(Anon)

246 From a children's exam: What is the meaning of R.I.P.?
Return If Possible.

247 From the same exam: Complete 'Where there's a will'...
There's a dead man.

I was intrigued to discover recently that the expression, 'He's gone for a Burton', was a wartime euphemism for an RAF pilot killed in action. It meant that the deceased was now drinking Burton's beer in the sky. Perhaps this epitaph from an earlier date refers to the original Burton himself:

248 A Brewer

Here lies poor Burton
He was both hale and stout
Death laid him on his bitter bier
Now in another world he hops about.

249 Here lies the body of Lester More
No Les, no More.

250 Wha lies here?
I, Johnny Doo.
Hoo, Johnny, is that you?
Ay, man, but a'm dead noo.

(Anon)

251 A wife had inscribed on her husband's tombstone:

'Thou art at rest—
Until we meet again.'

252 This calls to mind a brief exchange at a funeral:

Friend of the family: What were your father's last words?

Son: He didn't have any. My mother was with him to the end.

253 Then there was the man whose mother-in-law had died. He was asked by the undertaker, 'Do you want her cremated, buried or embalmed?'

He replied without hesitation: 'All three. Don't take any chances.'

254 The preacher was in full fury, describing the terrors of hell. 'There will be wailing and gnashing of teeth!' He boomed.

'Whaa abouh me?' called out a ninety-year-old heckler, 'I've goh no teef.'

The preacher thundered his reply: 'TEETH WILL BE PROVIDED!'

255 The poster read: 'Where will you be on the Day of Judgement?'

The graffiti artist had added: 'Still here waiting for the number 31 bus.'

256 The poster read: 'PREPARE TO MEET THY GOD'.
Underneath someone had scrawled the words: 'Evening Dress Optional.'

257 I heard recently of a second-hand car salesman whose last request was for the song 'I did it my way' to be sung at his funeral. Perhaps it should have been slightly adapted to: 'I did everyone my way.'

258 The Reverend Peter Lawrence has sent me three accounts of his experience conducting funerals. He has kindly allowed me to quote his vivid descriptions in full:

'A few years ago I was asked to take a burial service at Witton Cemetery. This is part of my job as an Anglican Vicar so although I did not know the deceased man I readily agreed.

'On the morning of the funeral I was ill. Rotten flu, foul cold. I tried to be brave. I forced myself out of bed, struggled into my dog collar and a few items of dark cloth, and drove to the cemetery. On the way I realised I needed a loo but, as there was not a lot of time to spare, I decided to wait until I reached the vestry.

'I drove around to the back of the chapel and parked by the ministers' door. Coughing and spluttering, robe over one arm, I secured the car, then grabbed the black vestry door knob firmly with my right hand. It had just been painted. There was no sign. It was still wet. The palm of my hand was now completely black.

' "I'll see to it inside," I thought and entered. No cloth. No towels. I was desperate for the toilet. No loo. My throat was dry and I couldn't stop coughing. No water.

'I heard the hearse pulling up outside. It is not easy putting on a cassock and surplice left-handed in a hurry. I did my best. It was a rushed job. I was aware I had messed up my hair completely in the process. No mirror.

'I struggled out, just as I was. My voice became weaker as the service went on. I tried not to gesticulate too much with my right hand. I would have given anything for a glass of water. I got through the service somehow and we all made our way to the graveside. I tried not to look too longingly at the trees we passed.

'Suddenly I was gripped with horror at the thought of the final blessing. Normally I hold up my right hand with my palm facing the mourners, in true evangelical style. That wouldn't do. I realised the need for an instant change in churchmanship.

'As the coffin was lowered I stood there with legs crossed, hair like a haystack, surplice slipping off one shoulder, voice nearly gone, eyes watering with discomfort. I made the sign of the cross in high-church style, right-handed with my palm facing sideways. I was careful to make sure the congregation only saw the white edge of my hand.

'I'd done it. I'd got away with it all. Everything was fine. I'd have been perfectly all right if the chief mourner had not come up to me and said, "What a moving service that was. Thank you so much. I must shake you by the hand."

'In my relief that the service was over, I grasped her right hand firmly in mine.'

259 'On another occasion,' the Reverend Lawrence writes, 'I took a funeral at Yardley Cemetery with a guest organist playing. I did my best. I said the same things I always say. Afterwards the lady organist stopped me. "What a lovely service," she sighed. "I am sure the family will have taken great comfort from everything you said."

' "Yes" agreed the Funeral Director, who was going past at the time, "I've been working here for thirty years and we haven't buried a sinner yet." '

260 Peter Lawrence's last story is my favourite: 'I did a burial about fourteen years ago at Lodge Hill Cemetery. There was only one mourner: a middle-aged man.

' "Right," I thought to myself. "It makes no difference. He will have the full service I always give."

'I thanked God for the life of the lady who had died. I allowed an appropriate moment of silence in which we could both remember and give thanks, and left nothing out.

'The grave was close to the chapel so the one mourner and I walked together behind the coffin. Eventually he broke the reverent silence.

' "No one could stand her," he said. "Terrible woman. We drew straws about who should come and I lost." '

261 My friend, the actor Stuart Harrison, overheard this recently in his local hospital:

Nurse: (Holding telephone and talking to the doctor) 'No...I'm afraid there's no answer from the mortuary.'

262 Here lies John Knott:
His father was Knott before him.
He lived Knott, died Knott,
Yet underneath this stone doth lie
Knott christened, Knott begot,
And here he lies and still is Knott.

(Anon)

263 A graduate of Trinity College, Cambridge, went through his life trading on his good connections. 'I'm a Trinity chap, you know,' was his favourite catchphrase. Doors were opened, club membership came easily. His business dealings were unethical and his private life a web of deceptions, but wherever he went—in the City or at fashionable cocktail parties or in exclusive golf clubs—he charmed his way through, pulling strings and mentioning the old college. Promotion came his way, respect and many honours.

Eventually he died, ennobled, a famous society figure with a full-page obituary in The Times. Standing outside heaven's gate, he knocked confidently. An angel peered over.

'I say—open up!' he called.

'I'm sorry, we don't have your name down,' explained the angel politely.

'It must be an error,' the man replied, 'I'm a Trinity chap, you know...check the list!'

The angel thumbed through the Book of Life. 'No, I'm sorry.'

'Now, *look here!*' The man was becoming extremely angry. Hearing the commotion, the Lord himself arrived.

'Ah, good,' said the man, 'now we'll get something done.'

The Lord shook his head sadly. 'It's strange I don't know you,' he said—'I'm something of a Trinity chap myself.'

264 Swans sing before they die—'twere no bad thing
Should certain persons die before they sing.
(Samuel Taylor Coleridge)

265 The world is a very dangerous place—you never get out of it alive.

266 I heard this story a long time ago and have no idea which holy man it refers to—but the incident has a refreshing, down-to-earth quality. Disciples were gathered reverently at the deathbed of the saint. The wise old man beckoned weakly. They leant forward, eager to hear his last words of wisdom which would guide them forward in their lives. What he said was: 'I could just do with a veal and ham pie.'

I have decided that this anonymous saint must have been the Blessed William Bunter of Greyfriars—no doubt famed for The Miracle of The Holy Tuckbox...

267 According to a local radio station, funerals in Sussex are the most expensive in Britain. The reason, it is claimed, is the high cost of living in the South-East.

268 A Methodist minister and a Catholic priest were great rivals in the village. They died on the same day and arrived in heaven. The Methodist was delighted to see that hundreds of Methodists were gathered round the throne of God. Beyond them, in an outer circle, were Church of England Christians, then other denominations in wider and wider circles—Baptists, Presbyterian, United Reformed. The circles stretched a long way. But far, far beyond them all—over the horizon—were the Catholics.

'What do you make of *that* then?' said the Methodist, triumphantly. But the priest seemed perfectly happy with this arrangement. 'Aren't you shocked?'

'Not at all,' said the priest, 'it's just been explained to me by the Archangel Gabriel. Apparently, mine are the only lot God can trust out of his sight.'

269 My great-aunt Ellie, who is featured in *Rolling in the Aisles*, had a fund of bizarre religious anecdotes. She would tell these stories gleefully, with an unforgettable cackle of laughter. Her laugh was even more outrageous than her stories, and I spent much of my childhood trying to perfect an imitation of that sound: something like a cross between the Laughing Policemen and a parrot going berserk.

She once told me how she had accidentally turned up at a spiritualist meeting, which was taking place in a former Baptist chapel. She was the visiting speaker for a missionary event a few doors further down the street but, instead of leaving in confusion as most people would have done, she decided to stay for a few minutes. Not only did she stay, but she decided to enquire after her husband.

'Your husband is in a very peaceful and happy place,' she was told. 'He comforts himself with the thought that one day you will be joining him.'

'I will be joining him—in a couple of hours,' she said, to the total astonishment of the spiritualists. 'Right now he's at home having a cup of tea and reading the newspaper.'

Auntie Ellie then swept out of the door and went cackling up the street to her missionary prayer meeting.

270 Auntie Ellie was always doing good to someone, somewhere. She regularly invited odd-looking people, the lame ducks and misfits of the world, in for tea. When the Bible speaks of 'God calling a peculiar people' to himself, I think it must be referring to Auntie Ellie and her friends.

She was one of those hyperactive characters who had a great fear of being bed-ridden. I remember her saying that it was her prayer to die standing on her feet. It seems that the prayer was answered. When the doctor called, on a routine visit, he found the kettle still boiling, and Ellie lying peacefully on the kitchen floor where she had fallen. I like to think that the Lord suddenly appeared and said: 'Ellie, today you're coming to *my* house for tea.'

271 My great-aunt's mild eccentricities pale beside the achievements of Mr Ernest Digweed, whose last will and testament can claim to be one of the most theologically challenging documents of the century. His case was reported in full in the *Daily Mail*, under the banner headline: '20 "Christs" claim £30,000'.

Twenty people are claiming to be Jesus and the rightful heir to £30,000 left in the will of religious recluse Ernest Digweed.

Mr Digweed was found dead four years ago in a tent in the living room of his home in Portsmouth. The walls were covered in crosses. He also lived sometimes under piles of deckchairs.

He left his entire estate to Jesus, so that He would have some money if the Second Coming should actually occur.

But until then, Mr Digweed named the Public Trustees as executors and it is they who must decide whether any of the claimants is Jesus.

They refuse to reveal the identities of the hopefuls, though one is rumoured to be a steelworker from Sheffield.

And they will not say what their criteria are for checking each claim.

An official said: 'We have politely acknowledged all claims. Usually people go away after a while or admit they cannot support the claim.

'If, however, there was a claim which appeared to be theologically sound, then it would have to be considered very carefully.'

THE TWINKLING OF AN EYE

(First quoted in Red Letter Days *by Paul Burbridge and Murray Watts, as the inspiration for a sketch on the Second Coming by Paul Burbridge)*

Index

Please note that numbers indicate joke numbers, not page numbers

Absent-mindedness 38, 130
Advice 90

Belief 225, 226
Bible reading 116-9
Bigamy 205
Bishops 12
Body Shop 241
Boredom 29
Bread 82
Bullets 70
'Buts' 128

Cannibalism 184
Cherubim 229
Children 5, 6, 7, 17, 239
Christian books 73, 219
Church 1, 2
Church attendance 231
Church buildings 10
Churchspeak 237
Clergy 21

Commandments 173
Commitment 96
Complacency 224
Constantine, Sir
    Leary 46
Creation 3
Cricket 14
Criticism 86
Crop circle watchers 80
Culture Shock 232, 233
Curates 33, 201

Death 242, 266
Devil 91
Direction 93
Dogma 81
Drink 179, 182

Epitaphs 243-5, 248-51, 262
Equality 101, 197
Ethics 180
Euphemisms 7, 235

Evangelists 61
Evidence 181
Evil 15
Excuses 175
Exorcism 63

False worship 228
Feast of Fools 207
Food 234
Fools 92
Funerals 252, 253,
    257-60, 267

Gifts of the Spirit 67
Gospel song 64
Gossip 85
Graffiti 83, 220, 255, 256

Harvest 13, 218
Haste 211, 212
Healing 72, 74, 75
Heaven 263, 270
Hecklers 30
Hell 206, 254
Howlers 131-170, 246,
    247
Human nature 172
Husbands 103, 187-9,
    192, 194, 202
Hymns 238, 240

Insults 102

Keeping score 99

Life 88
Limericks 45
Lord's Day Observance
    Society 178
Love 98
Lying 177

Mahaffy, Dr 37
Majari Maharaj Ji 76
Men 204
Methodists 268
Middle-age 222
Ministry 214-221
Misprints 104, 106-15
Mistakes 125
Money 52-61
Morality 171
Mortuary 261
Mothers 9, 208

Noah 91
Normal family life 227
Notices 62
Nursery rhymes 68, 69

Ornithology 80

Pearls before swine 31
Pessimists 89
Piety 176, 185
Plagiarism 27
Politicians 79
Praise 11

Prayer, children's 16, 47, 51
  desperate 42
  general 48, 49
  in extremis 50
  Irish 41
  Parliamentary 43
  self-serving 44
Preachers 25, 28, 32, 36, 40, 120-24, 174
Prison 100
Progress 213
Proposals 191
Psychologists 210

Quarrels 223

Religion 97
Repentance 84
Roman Catholics 230
Royle, Roger 65

St Christopher 183
Schizophrenia 209
Self-control 87

Sermons 18-24, 26, 27, 35, 37, 39
Services 34
Slogans 215-217, 265
Smith, Bishop Sidney 33
Smoking 8
Spirit, Holy 71
Spiritualism 77, 78, 269
Swans 264

Temperance 186
Tongues 66
Trinity 263
Twins 4

Ugly faces 129

Watson, David 126, 127, 236
Weddings 105, 190, 199, 200
Wills 271
Wisdom 94, 95
Wives 193, 195, 196, 198, 203